Mia and Anthony and The Hidden Treasures

Treasure Number Two –
A Million Ways to Care

About the Author

Joe Khoury writes on topics that are important to him; on core values that he hopes would inspire, educate and enlighten his children, step-children and hopefully others.

In 2019 he found a few precious notes in his mother's handwriting; Having lost both his parents while so young, he realized that he didn't really know much about them: what were their likes, dislikes, hopes, fears and even points of view on certain topics? He decided to begin writing so that – in the event that something should happen to him, my children and even future grandchildren would be able to know the core values and life lessons he hopes for them to learn.

Learn more about the author and the characters by visiting our website at lessonsformykidsbooks.com or scan the QR Code below

Anthony and Mia are having fun playing on the floor with their toys while Mom and Dad watch the TV news. The twins aren't watching TV because the news is usually very boring. Cartoons are much more fun!

Today is different, though! The children stop playing and watch when a wonderful news story appears. A very, very rich man has given a MILLION DOLLARS to help build a new hospital in a poor, African country.

"Wow! He's so kind!" said Mia.

"Yes, he is," agreed Dad.

"I wish I could be that kind," said Anthony, "but I've only got one dollar. That wouldn't pay for much."

"No," giggled Mia. "That wouldn't even buy one brick for the hospital."

"Oh, well." Anthony sighed. "It would be nice to be rich, though, because I'd like to be kind."

"But you don't need to be rich to be kind," said Dad.

"No," added Mom. "It was very nice of that man to give so much money, but kindness is just about caring for other people. That means the tiniest bit of kindness is just as important as what that man has done."

"Anyway, children. It's time for bed," said Dad, turning off the TV.

"Come on, Anthony," said Mia. "Let's tidy our toys away and go upstairs."

After Mom and Dad had tucked them into bed, Anthony called to Mia.

"Do you think that's true, Mia? Do you think little bits of kindness are important?"

"I'm not sure, Anthony. Maybe only millionaires can be really kind." Mia yawned. "I'm tired. Goodnight, Anthony."

"Goodnight, Mia."

Downstairs, Mom was talking to Dad.

"It was so kind of the children to tidy away their toys. I've had such a hard day and have an awful headache. It's nice to know they care about me. Some children just leave their mess for Mom to tidy up and wouldn't tidy up even if you offered them a MILLION DOLLARS."

The next morning, Dad was sitting in the kitchen when Mia when Anthony ran in from the garden.

"Dad! Can we go to help Louise, please?" asked Anthony. "She's trying to plant some trees, but they're big and heavy. I'm worried she'll hurt herself!"

Dad put his shoes on, and off they went. Louise smiled when she saw help arriving.

Anthony tried to carry a tree by himself, but it was too big. Mia couldn't carry her tree, either.

"Don't worry," said Dad. "If we all work together, we'll soon have these planted."

"Gosh! I wish I was stronger, Louise," said Anthony.

"Yes," said Mia. "If we were big and strong, we could help more."

"Look around!" said Louise, turning to look up and down the street. "No one else has come to help me. You have, though, and that makes you big and strong enough for me!"

After they finished and were walking home, Anthony turned to Dad. He was confused.

"What did Louise mean when she said we were big and strong, Dad? We're just two little children."

"Well," said Dad. "She was struggling all by herself, so she felt really good when you came to help."

"But we weren't strong enough to do as much as we wanted, Dad," said Mia.

"The important thing is that Louise didn't feel all on her own anymore," said Dad. "You showed that you care about her, and that means a lot."

"Not as much as a MILLION DOLLARS," said Anthony.

"You don't know that," said Dad. "When you're kind to people, it's always worth more to them than you think."

As they walked away, Louise looked at her lovely new trees. She was so happy.

"Come on, you two," said Mom when they got home. "You're dirty after all that hard work, and you need to wash and get changed. It's your friend's party today, remember."

When they arrived at the party, Anthony and Mia were excited to see their friends.

"Hello, Stella! Hello, Hazel!" they said happily.

Just before they ran over to their friends, Mom pointed across the room.

"Look at the girl standing all by herself," she said "Imagine if you went to a party and didn't know anyone. You'd want people to say hello to you, wouldn't you?"

"Of course," said Mia.

"Yes," said Anthony. "We want people to be kind to us, so we should be kind to other people."

Just then, a boy they didn't know went up to the girl.

"Ha! Ha! You look silly," he said. "Why are you dressed like that? It's dumb!"

The girl was wearing a long, blue dress and had a white scarf wrapped around her head.

"That's not nice," said Mia. "Come on, Anthony." The twins went over to the girl.

"Hello, I'm Anthony and this is Mia. What's your name?"

"I'm Layla," replied the girl. "I've just moved here with my family."

"I love your clothes," said Mia.

"I dress like this because I'm a Muslim," replied Layla.

"Wow! That's interesting," said Anthony. "What does that mean?"

Layla was shy at first but soon started telling the twins all about her culture and religion.

Then the twins invited Layla to play with them and their friends. Soon, Layla was friends with Stella and Hazel. Then Cole and Olivia arrived at the party and joined in the fun.

On the way home after the party, Mom was in a good mood.

"You were really kind to Layla, today," she said. "You made her feel very welcome." "Oh, I didn't know we were being kind, Mom," said Mia. "We just wanted Layla to be happy."

"That's what being kind is," said Mom. "It's caring for other people."

"That's cool," said Anthony. "We can all care about each other, can't we? It doesn't cost anything."

In another car, Layla was talking to her Mom on the way home from the party.

"I'm so happy I've made friends, Mom," she said.

"So am I," said her Mom. "You've been crying yourself to sleep every night since we moved here. I know you miss your old friends, but you'll be happy now you've made some new ones."

"Yes… Mom, can we invite Mia and Anthony over to play, please?"

"Of course, and I'll make them something nice to eat. They were kind to you, so it will be nice for us to be kind to them."

When they got home, the twins were really tired. They'd worked hard in the garden and then gone to the party. It had been a busy day.

"Well, children," said Dad. "I hope you've said thank you to Mom for taking you to the party."

"Oops… thanks, Mom," said Anthony. "Thanks, Mom," said Mia.

"Well, thank you for being so polite," said Mom. "Right! It's time to go shopping for Christmas presents for the families from church.

"I'm too tired," groaned Mia. "Can we do it another day?"

"No, Mia," said Dad. "It's important we help those families to have a nice Christmas."

Mia and Anthony were tired, but they knew Dad was right. When they arrived at the mall, they soon cheered up and had a great time choosing gifts. They were really excited when they got home and started wrapping all the lovely presents.

But, then, Anthony noticed that Mia had stopped wrapping and was sitting with her eyes closed.

"What are you doing?" he asked.

"I'm imagining the children opening these presents on Christmas morning," she said.

Anthony grinned and closed his eyes, as well. He imagined a young boy and girl with happy, smiling faces on Christmas morning.

"Mom?" said Anthony. "Why is giving presents even more fun than getting them?"

"Because making someone happy is the best feeling in the world," said Mom. "It's worth.... Oh, I don't know... more than a MILLION DOLLARS!"

After they had taken the presents to church, the children were looking forward to going home. "Right! One more job to do today," said Mom.

"Oh, no! We're exhausted," moaned Anthony.

"Are you even too tired to buy flowers for your babysitter Veronique?" asked Dad. "Is it her birthday?" asked Mia.

"No," said Dad.

"Is she poor?" asked Anthony.
"No," said Mom.

"Then why are we buying her flowers?" asked Mia. "Can't we just go home? She doesn't need flowers."

"Well, let's think about it," said Mom. "She takes care of you, she's kind to you, she's a nice person, she's always there for you."

The children ran into the flower store and picked a beautiful bunch of bright yellow flowers.

"You've got a lovely store here!" said Mia to the store owner. The lady behind the counter smiled. She'd worked hard to make her store nice, and it made her happy when people noticed.

Just as they were leaving, a young boy came in with his Mom.

"Hola, Juan," said the twins.

"Hello, Anthony. Hello, Mia," said Juan with a smile.

"Well," said Dad as they walked to the car. "You two are full of surprises. I didn't know you could speak Spanish."

"Juan has moved here from Mexico and is in our class," explained Anthony.

"Yes," said Mia. "It's difficult for him to learn English," said Mia. "So, we asked him to teach us some Spanish."

"He really likes it when we say something in his language," said Anthony, "And it helps us to understand how tricky it can be for him to learn a language."

The Americas

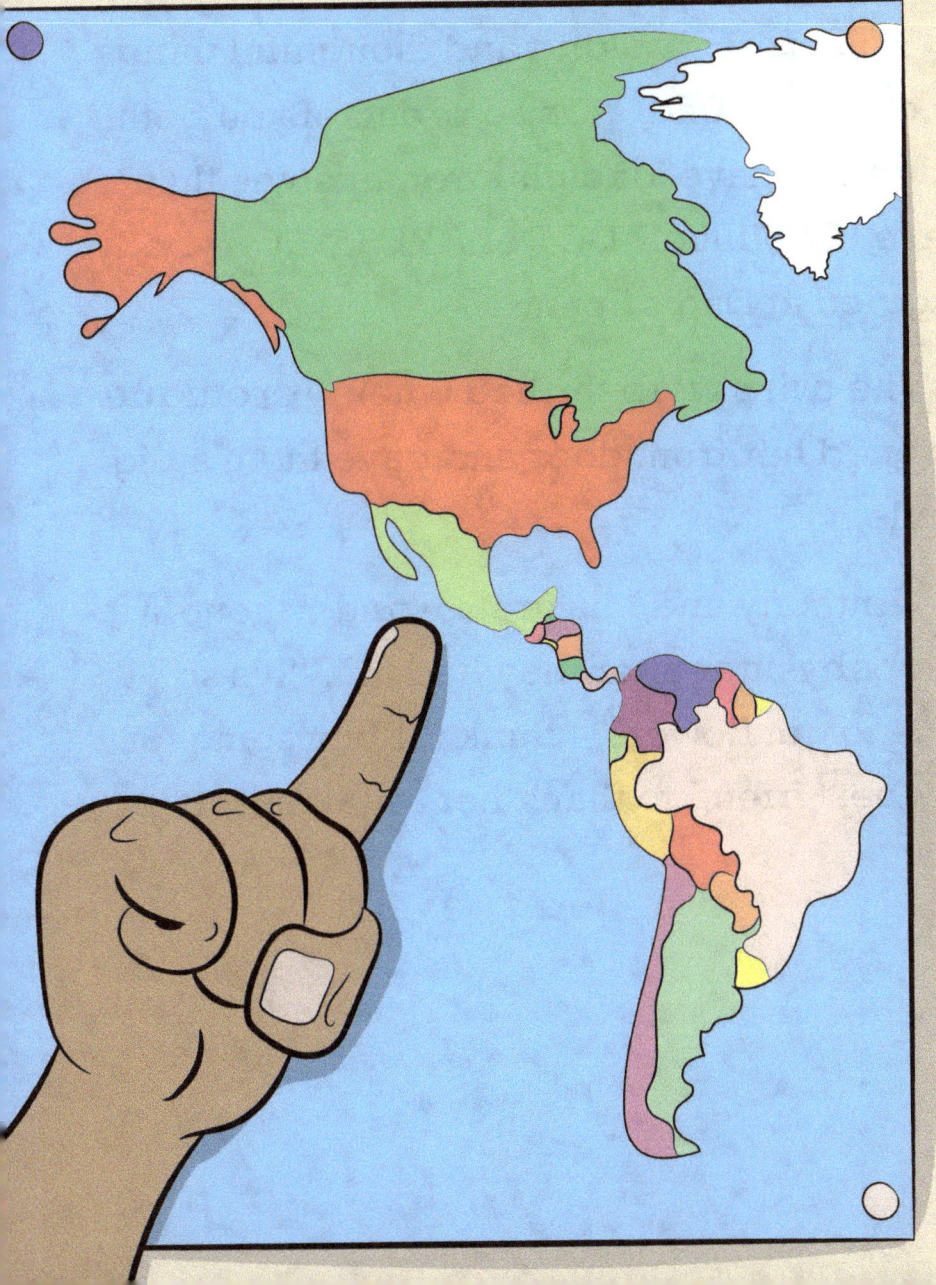

"That is such a kind and thoughtful thing to do," said Dad. "I'm so proud of you both. I'd rather have kind children like you than have UN MILLóN DE DóLARES." Everybody giggled at Dad's Spanish.

The twins were thrilled when Veronique opened her front door and gave them a big smile.

"Anthony and Mia are so kind," thought the babysitter after they had left. "It's so nice to get flowers. I think I'll buy some for my best friend to thank her for all her help."

So, that's exactly what she did.

Her friend was so happy with her flowers, she decided to buy some for her Mom. Her Mom was so pleased to get flowers, she bought some for her sister.

Her sister was so pleased, she bought some for her neighbor.

Anthony's and Mia didn't know it, but their little act of kindness grew and grew and made more and more people happy.

Both the twins were so happy when they got home. They'd had a busy day of gardening, parties, choosing presents and delivering flowers. Now, they just wanted to go to sleep.

Before climbing into bed, they knelt down to say their prayers. They thanked God for all the good things in their life, including Mom and Dad, their nice home, their school, and all their friends.

"And thank you for teaching me to be kind to people," said Mia.

"Yes, and for showing us that you don't need a MILLION DOLLARS to be kind." Said, Anthony. "It's the small things we do every day that are important."

Goodnight, Mia," said Anthony after prayers. "I really enjoyed today. I've been worried that I'm not good enough to be on the baseball team, but practicing kindness is more important than practicing baseball. I'm really happy I was kind to Louise and Veronique."

"I know," said Mia. "I've been worried about some of my grades at school, but I learned a big lesson outside of school today. I loved being kind to Layla and to the families from church." Mia yawned.

"Goodnight, Anthony… and thank you."

"What for?" asked Anthony.

"Well, it's nice to have a brother who's kind." Anthony laughed.

"Well, it's nice to have such a kind sister as well."

What have we learned?

- Treat all people with love and respect; from all races, religions and cultures.

- You don't need to be rich to be kind.

- When you're kind to people, it's always worth more to them than you think.

- Kindness is contagious: It will make other people want to bekind.

- Small acts of kindness go a long way: Saying thank you, picking up our toys, giving away toys we don't play with to kids with no toys...

Now go make the world a better place!

My Kindess Diary: